Beyond Rubies

Beyond Rubies
Tuesday Group Anthology

Edited by Ann Sansom

smith|doorstop

Published 2017 by
Smith|Doorstop Books
The Poetry Business
Bank Street Arts
32-40 Bank Street
Sheffield S1 2DS

ISBN 978-1-910367-74-2
Typeset by Camilla Lovell Design
Printed and bound by CPI Group (UK) Ltd, Croydon, CR0 4YY

Acknowledgements
Kath Lightfoot
Extract taken from *The House* (Smith|Doorstop)

Smith|Doorstop Books are a member of Inpress:
www.inpressbooks.co.uk. Distributed by NBN International, Airport
Business Centre, 10 Thornbury Road Plymouth PL 6 7PP

The Poetry Business receives financial support from Arts Council England.

Contents

For Kath Lightfoot
A genuine ruby

Dee Ashurst

Ghost Wish

Long gone is the fear of Old Nick appearing over your shoulder as
you sit at the mirror admiring the fluttering false eyelashes and
          bright green lipstick.
Now you can sit and do nothing for as long as you like, knowing the
          devil won't make use of idle hands,
go to bed long after eight o'clock without concern that Wee Willie
          Winnie will shout through the letter box.
And you can get straight into bed without first having to kneel on
the rabbit skin rug, hands together, eyes closed and shiver your way
          through all those God bless everybodys.
You can listen to the Salvation Army band without having to stop
fidgeting and sing up, enjoy your porridge with a thick layer of sugar
on top; pick Yorkshire puddings up with your fingers, eat with
elbows on the table, leave your shoes on when you come indoors
and use as many pegs on each item of clothing as you like when you
          hang them out to dry.
You can happily live your life on your own-ness, enjoy the
          contentment and do whatever you want.
But you'd love her ghost to visit you sometimes.

Knowledge

I know he has his own lorry now and takes women pea picking
I know why gangs of boys walk at the other side of the road
       They're scared of our Rinty
I know how he got water to shoot out of the pile of rocks to make a
       fountain in the garden
I don't know how Mr Wilson eats now he has a hole in the front of
       his neck
I know my mam says he has a nasty smell around him
I know drinking vinegar from the bottom of your chip paper rots
       your stomach
And that Ikey McGee got warts in his throat from daring to drink
       school ink
I don't know how she makes wax roses but I know people look
shocked when they pass our garden in winter and the roses are in
       full bloom
I know Marion Craggs has nits and that I'll be in trouble if I catch
       them
I know you can catch TB from people spitting in the street and you
       can die from it
I know how to say my prayers every night or I won't go to heaven
I know to keep away from Dirty Lucy's gate and to always
       remember my manners.

Night

Burglars, drug dealers and drunks are thankful for night.
John Lee, black hooded and silent
mobile phone lighting up his white face
as he supplements his giro. Buster at his heels.
The ambulance arrives at A&E with his unconscious mother.
A taxi drops Old Les at his gate. He wobbles up the path
and pees against his bin.
I watch till he's safe inside, close my curtains and go to bed.

Wash House

They shut the door on a cloud of steam.
They hadn't heard me come in and I closed the street door quietly.
They knew something.
I'd only told Biddy but news got round quickly in that wash-house
especially if Gladys was at the sinks, ears like bees wings that one.
Old Lila would keep her mouth shut, she had to, it was her living
but she only had to be seen talking to someone and tongues would
      start wagging.
Things seemed as usual as I hung up my shawl and went inside.

Mrs Blower was possing and wobbling as she went; Ginny and
Bertha were mangling and singing; skinny Winnie was scooping
water from the copper into a dolly tub and lazy Ada was having a
      fag in the corner.
I breathed a sigh of relief as I put my hands on my stomach and
walked across to my pile of sheets. Then, Ginny Longstaff sidled
across, leaned conspiratorially towards me and whispered 'You
      alright, ducks?'
It was then that I knew she knew.

Igloo

You won't remember that winter of deep snow,

how she'd muffled me up in wellies, coat, bonnet,
scarf and gloves with an extra pair of socks over them.

You showed me how to make snow into bricks, pile them up
and cement them together with more snow.

How we cleared a circle of snow big enough to fit us both inside.
It was the first time I had heard the word Igloo.

She came outside and gave us both a mug of hot Milo.
We spent a long time on the last bit, it kept falling in.

We took a cushion and the little cracket which grandad had made
and sat on them inside, and you brought his bike lamp.

It was dark and magical but not for long. The roof kept falling in
so we sat around the edges.

It began to snow again and she had made rabbit stew for dinner.
But you won't remember.

And if I knew you would visit my mind

I wouldn't even try to get some kind of order in there
I would let you in the back door and leave through the front

closing that door behind me for a while.
You would come across problems of every kind:

a variety of mental health concerns, sift through worries
and traumas, nightmares, memories and false beliefs

only to find that they don't belong to me.
I'm just holding them for other people.

Susan Bedford

Reading H is for Hawk *by Helen Macdonald*

I feel it will work out
in the end, including the death.
If there is one.

The birds are happy, I need to believe that.
I've admired them at fairs, perched.
I've wished I could have one on my clenched fist.

I've looked at their feathers at close quarters,
wanted to stroke them, as if they were family pets,
with their wings clasped to their sides.

There's a few inches of leather between a foot and the perch –
all that is needed for them to know not to bother,
all that is needed for them to know the invisible cage

that stands between them and their sky.
We can, it seems, with tried and tested methods,
subdue them, get them to come back for us,

stand low for us, let us look them in the eye.
For enough raw chicks, we can have them in our world,
believe that we have a bond

between the powerful and the overpowered,
like we have everything,
and are used to it.

Helen puts the hood over its exhausted head,
takes away the sitting room, the ceiling,
that does for a leafy canopy.

The Guest Room

The silver chalice, and the rhinoceros from my mum,
the *Dark Side of the Moon* that I played at Anne's party,
not to mention the shelf of old novels,
and the dog psychology book that I thought would tell me
            something new,
and the overspill from my study. Well if you have a sleepless night,
or feel up to a spot of psychology yourself, or the Divine Office,
you're not short of material here. A Teasmade would be nice too:
I'll enquire as to your favourite tea. And a bed jacket. I make do with
            a fleece,
but I have had two bed jackets in my time: one Margaret's
            mum made,
one from the Grattan catalogue – yellow with a brown trim, that
            turned out to be see-through –
that my mum said I could *not wear* when the doctor came.
I didn't like it myself but I had to see it through. Like the Vesta
            Chow Mein.
I'll get out the hot water bottle, or would you like the heating left on?
People are very particular about bedroom heating. I'll explain about
the shower and the do's and don'ts regarding the alarm,
since that man walked into the bedroom in a balaclava, but that
            won't happen while you're here.

The Industrial North

On the top of the No 11 my mum says that it was alright for our
    Peter,
but that girls don't go to university.

The club turn sings The Impossible Dream, and by the end of
    the night
we are dancing round the tables

and on Monday I'm conjugating Latin verbs and deciphering
    hieroglyphics.
My brother says I'm a snob, which has something to do with my
    boyfriend

who does cookery, which also makes him a poof.
And the cello and the briefcase.

It would be ok if I left and went to be an over-locker at Cohen
    and Wilks,
but a subtle seismic shift routes him one way and me another.

Monastery

I know it will be like going home,
except not my people, my colours, my dog,
but I belong there. I know it's not easy,

and you're pared down,
and sometimes you could murder someone,
and it's not as quiet as you'd hoped. Or as temporary.

In the Monastery Chapel

the tallest candlestick I have ever seen
with the Paschal candle on top,
and us in a circle round it, after a procession
referred to by a Brother as liturgical musical chairs.

So we stand, hearing ancient chant and ancient readings.
We could be in the fourth century, these postures,
this incense. This waiting.

Now it's dark and we file out
past, off-stage, the tallest step ladder I have ever seen,
back to our rooms by torch-light in silence
to a night.

Psalm Of Those Who Walk Dogs in the Park

With my whole heart I will give thanks for the dogs and the dog walkers and the paths of the park: the paths are long and straight. How can we count the paths?

In the midst of the park the dog walkers talk one to another: the dogs and the breeze are the words on their lips. Oh how much is the breeze on their lips. They say one to another Hello and Look at
    your dog.

For many years have the dogs and dog walkers walked the paths: though they may walk in the midst of trouble they are refreshed on the paths. I will slay my enemies who seek to destroy these paths.

How good and joyful are the dogs and their walkers on these paths. They are like precious ointment upon the head: this shall be their place for ever. Here will they walk and have delight therein.

Kathryn Cross

La Vietnamienne, 1982

'Bonjour Alain. C'est Joanne, d'Angleterre. Ça va?'
Alain says 'Oui' but little else; he's only seven. I say, 'Linh, elle est là?'
He says you're in your room and he will fetch you. I hear his slow,
exaggerated footsteps on the steep wooden staircase that leads to
your attic room as he goes to tell you, his adopted sister, to come to
the phone. My thoughts find you, while I wait.

You'll be sitting on your bed. With bracelets jangling, you'll have just
executed a perfect one-handed cigarette roll. With your free hand,
you'll have picked up an opened book of French poetry, pushed
your little round glasses back onto the bridge of your nose and
recommenced reading. You'll have reminded yourself to make notes
of any words you don't understand.

On the table by the bed there'll be a straw coloured tisane cooling
in a delicate china bowl. You'll be in jeans, a thin cotton blouse and
you'll be moving your bare feet to some traditional jazz tumbling out,
playful and earnest, from the cassette player on the floor.

When you got up this morning you'll have rinsed your waist length
hair in the Indian rosewater you buy every week from the grocery in
the village. Heady and sweet, it's an intoxicating aroma of centuries
of ceremony, blessings and births. But for me, it is your smell; it
evokes you and all that is yours.

Outside your attic window a parched Provencal hillside will be
teeming with insect life. I remember last summer when a dragonfly
glided in to rest on a papier-mâché box on the table by your bed. I
asked to see what was inside the box, so you gently waved the insect
away and opened it. There were rings, hair bands, notes written in

Vietnamese, pressed flowers, and, in a small envelope, a photograph of a smartly dressed couple. They were your parents, you said with eyes cast down.

I had so many questions about Saigon, about the boats, about the refugees, but you closed the lid, put the box back on the table. You never spoke of it.

I can hear Alain coming back down the stairs. You'll have put down your book, taken off your glasses and, after rubbing tired eyes, got up from the bed, picked up the tisane and made your way towards the door. Now your quiet but purposeful steps bring you to the phone.

On the Bridge

Our Boston train, New York its goal, snakes on the eastern seaboard.
Over from London, first time in the States, I sit facing forward.
About half way, the train slows and I'm seduced by a familiar place.
But I'm drunk on New World history and all those copycat names.

On Thames River Bridge we wait outside New London, city and port.
Its harbour, a majestic millpond; the best of British, brought
over the pond, made brighter, fresher, bluer, calmer; super sized.
I conjure a settler's boast, 'Look, Ma'am even quaint is done in style.'

I'm hooked. It's beautiful, tranquil, and there'd be money here, enough.
I could bring a piece of my London with me, leaving behind all
         that stuff.
Could this place shake me up, get me in gear? Get me to start anew?
Washed in these magical waters, could I be a new version too?

Or I could wake up and smell the coffee on the approaching cart!
As the train sets off, jolting me back to myself, I resolve to start
sorting out all that stuff; change my own gears, wash myself clean.
No maritime alchemy here. Just a brush with the American dream.

Warping Drain

after waiting, that thrill
a disappearing float
rod bending
toward a big fish

fantasizing he's a star
on Match Day, with photo op
hair combed, grinning
a twelve pound carp in capable hands

curses litter the bank, a snapped line
is a gunshot sometimes
sub-standard gear, poor planning,
or just bad luck

but he's still in the game
kneeling down to tie on
a new hook, add fresh bait
if Warping Drain means anything

there'll be other fish, new thrills

Almost You

At first I saw you everywhere in the daily run of things.
You sat across from me on the tube in highly polished brogues.
Had you thrown out your trainers?

One day you were sweeping up leaves in the park,
near my digs, sporting a beard.
It didn't suit you, love.

You were on the same train as me going back up north
wearing a suit and tie.
Where were the jeans, the T-shirts?

I saw you in a café shouting at a waiter.
But you'd never do that; you're an introvert
and besides – 'we're all oppressed,' you'd say.

I saw you every day for weeks
until I gave up waiting, gave up looking,
and then you vanished.

Feeding Time

'John, was it a good idea to tell them you'd rinsed the spinach in the bath?'

'There was so much of the blinking stuff, Carol. I didn't have a bowl big enough.'

'But did you have to mention it?'

'I was nervous. It just came out.'

'No one finished the soup after that, though, did they?'

'Er ... no. Sorry love.'

Tim thinks they talk rubbish. A load of 'yackety-yack'. And it's boring. He'd rather stare out of the window at this summer's hit — a bird feeder dangling from a fancy hook against his dad's garage. All week six young blue tits no bigger than conkers have darted between next door's tree and a fat-ball feast. Colourful acrobats, wings flapping in fast-forward, take their turn to hang upside down from the swinging plastic cage. Squeaking sounds come from beaks as tiny as the bits of seed they grab, while, every couple of seconds, fluffy heads swivel round to keep a beady, baby eye on life in the garden.

They are brilliant. And they do all this at a thousand heart beats per minute. Tim learned this at school.

'John, I hope you cleaned the bath out first ... '

'About that, Carol ... '

'Yackety-yack'. He'll watch his birds all day. Long after the stupid soup has gone cold.

Alex Goss

Window

On the sill, dirty plates where the basil towered, taken back to uni.
The window frames green, beeches, self-set sycamores, a cold bonfire.
To the right, flaming Virginia creeps through the grass to the shot
   lettuces.
Mr Matthews creeps too, around the bushes.
He thinks there won't be anyone in at this time on a Sunday
   morning.
The Tesco lorry beeps, reversing up the kerb.

Derryoge

It fell to Betty and Nana to clear out Derryoge. No one else had the heart for it, though all admitted it had to be done. New roof, rewiring, the garden much too big for Opa now. Alec was in hospital, sectioned during one of his hypomanic phases. They heard from the McMinns that it was for sale.

So no one complained when Betty burnt the photographs. Betty hated photographs. The furniture was sent to auction.

A few pieces were taken to the new house at Sydenham. The neat writing bureau, the sleigh bed, the smaller armchairs. A modern cooker was needed. Would Nana ever get used to the electric plates after the old gas range?

Alec got the rotary bookcase with the numbered Penguins but no one had room for the long mahogany one, with the philosophy, poetry – sets of Dickens and Shakespeare, Robbie Burns. He lamented the globe – so much better than an atlas for young minds; and it was gone. Sally grieved over the pianos. And the long kitchen table made from a single piece of oak, where Opa sat to eat his porridge, when he emerged, at leisure in his later years. It went for ten shillings.

No one could take the bathroom, big enough to move in, the large rectangular sink, the pedestal bath, the tiles and gleaming linoleum in cream and black.

Sometimes he'd wake and think about if he'd been himself and had the money. How the weeins would run in and out through the wide hall, banging the gong and pulling the bell, by the study fireplace. The doors open to the terraces in summer, the path through the rhododendrons to the lawn and the vegetable garden on the right, down to the orchard. Opa's peas were the sweetest – he put lime in the soil.

Apples. Nana repeated often, how Alec loved apples. Back in Elswick Street when he was only a tot he would say, 'I know you've got apples, for I can smell them.' Later Jim would climb the trees and throw the apples to the prisoners working on the railway. He couldn't see them but 'Danke Schön' came over the tall hedges.

One December night during the war, a consignment of turkeys arrived at the front door. And then boxes of greyhound covers. No one knew anything about it except that it would be something to do with Alec, now in the RAF. Sure enough, he turned up a couple of days later with a van to transport the lot to Nutts Corner to fly back to Lincolnshire. Christmas presents for the officers and men. Just some of the stories of Derryoge, now a coterie of shops with a by-pass behind.

Connection

My Dad, Alec, worked night shifts at the telephone exchange in May Street. He loved to play along with callers he knew, letting slip facts about them, or those he thought he might know or would like to know, seeking a connection. He addressed them as 'caller'. 'Hold the line caller!', 'Madam' or 'Sir'. Sometimes this would be for show if he were in hearing of the supervisor and arranging a free call to me in the nurses' home.

One night he had a request for a trunk call from a phone box in Donegal. It was my mother's distant relative, Aunt Jane Savage, trying to contact my Aunt Roberta McGrath. She had no telephone number, nor the address. He asked the caller, 'Would Mrs McGrath keep the odd pig and chicken? Would that be Mrs McGrath, of Ballyclare, the Achadowey bowling champion? Is Mrs McGrath one of ten; nine girls and a boy?' He played along releasing snippets till at last Aunt Jane declared, 'I know who you are!'

Some mornings he would go home via the Peter Pan bakery at the Knock Road lights, to get a crusty loaf, later a soft loaf, potato farls and a newspaper or two. Then a mile's walk home. If it was raining stair rods he rode the bus to the terminus up at Gilinahirk and down again. God help the driver who had nothing to say.

When Frances was living in The Orchard he would call in on his way home and toss rashers of bacon and potato bread on her kitchen island, saying 'Would you throw that in a pan, Frances?' She with two young children, a barrister husband and a household to run.

Some nights he finished at 11. If he'd stopped at Ballyhackamore for a drink at Paddy Lamb's, he'd come in and turn on all the lights in our bedrooms 'to see who was in'.

Where did he think we'd be, schoolgirls at midnight?

One night he was chatting to a fellow-worker who happened to be leaning against a pillar. A small puff of plaster dust fell on the colleague's shoulder. They tutted at the state of Telephone House. When it happened twice more, they realised it was a sniper. With all the barricades and bullet-proof glass, someone had left a window open to the hub of communication for Northern Ireland. It fascinated Alec that the sniper was traced to Short Strand nearly a mile away and that the gunman had managed to aim his shot through the slit of a partly opened window.

He carried a cheap pigskin briefcase with newspapers, tea leaves and a small whiskey bottle containing milk. He wore a Columbo style raincoat and a trilby. With his NHS plain spectacle frames and his general build, his colleagues named him 'Harry Worth', whom coincidentally, he adored, along with Bilko, Steptoe, Laurel and Hardy and other innocent anarchists. When his psychiatrist, Dr McCluggage, was establishing rapport, something my father was always happy to do, they were discussing television. When Dr McCluggage said, 'Bilko's a darling', Alec was sold. It had taken four male nurses to hold him down to administer the injection that knocked him out.

Today he would be labelled 'bi-polar' though he was perpetually up rather than down. The only times he was depressed was when he was hospitalised and given ECT and Largactil.

When he lost his licence, and other jobs, he got to know the bus times and the drivers, the rhythm of his later life.
Sometimes I wish we were still out on the harbour at Portnablagh swimming from the steps after a hot day, trying not to fall out of our bikinis. Shelley and Sharon prepubescent splashing amongst the gleaming boats of the beautiful people. Sometimes I wish we were thirteen again.

Alex Goss   31

Ducking

With the span of his hand
He pushes the boy's head
Like a basket ball
Under he goes
And up again
Under and up
All in good fun
The pretty woman holds a baby
Looks away
Under and up again

Entrance Exam

I lit a candle for you today. What else could I do?
I got you into this not quite believing that friends are all
    that matter.
Brilliant fragile flower among the confident boys with the
    smart mothers.

In the Suburb

In the suburb on the Roman ridge in the largest county,
don't try to imagine, it's not that simple,
this is the rain that wasn't forecast
these are the gas pipes, these the labourers
these are the barriers, the temporary traffic lights

This is the roundabout
See the posse of people
This is the cash machine where they park, unable to walk
This is the chain store corner shop
These are the staff who notice if you've not been in
who send you a card if you're sick
Who lend you a trolley

This is the church where you can go if you want
to join in with how it's always been done
This is the woman who buys sherry every day
These are the dog walkers on the central reservation

Angela O'Connor

It happens regularly

It's always the same, usually on a pay night.
The lime coloured van carefully enters the driveway.
Never any damage done to the bougainvillea.

I steal a look from behind the nylon curtains.
Gauge my performance for the next few hours.
Deliberate steps hold the banister too tight.

Fumbling keys and unrelenting locks accompanied with
familiar sworn statements, confirm my expectation.
Be good, sit quiet, say hello and act like normal – the drill.

He's drunk, very very drunk, it's Thursday night drunk.
The aroma of Marlboro and beer hits me hard.
Before his lop-sided smile tries to harness his shadow.

Dinner eaten in silence, interrupted only by his bodily functions.
I pray to myself – who else will listen; 'please have a bath, please
have a bath'. Hoping the hot waters may assuage any fight within.
I lay awake to hear his cleansed but heavy footsteps carry him
away to his version of dreamland.
And now I go to mine, thankful and yet anxious of the next time.

Freycinet

Freycinet so far away but everyday I see you.
Your wineglass bay looks at me whenever I close my distant eyes.
Golden sunset, white sands and ice cold water.
The Antarctic winds never mimic another.
Bountiful land I love you so. Untouched by man –
unfortunately no. Still you are here, for all to see;
Freycinet never that far away.

Four Days

Forgotten four days; those last hours of May.
Lunch at Lo Sfizio Di Bianchi, al fresco
in the sun-drenched cobblestone courtyard.

The orange fizz of bitter aperol leads onto a fine classico
from the local enoteca. Pane con sale, huge juicy tomatoes drizzled
with luxurious green gold. Buffalo mozzarella oozed its treasure

as your fingers tore it apart. You reminded me of a child
discovering food for the first time. Ecstasy.
We walked through the vineyards close to your home.

Chianti white soil marked by boar and deer. Natural wine
        predators.
I picked the sangiovese, plump and firm. You didn't, you knew
        better.
Fields upon fields of black eyed red poppies shone such happiness

not remembrance of pain. Swallows danced in the sky.
Breathtakingly diving headlong into the pool for a morsel of aqua.
Fragile yet fierce. Four unforgettable days. Another four days is all
        I want.

Then and Now

The party starts at nine. It's seven forty-five already. I haven't washed my hair. Panic sets in. Fifteen minutes to wash, about twenty to dry, then make-up, shit I don't even know what I'll wear.

'Just put on that wool jersey tunic, you know the green one, or what do you call it, 'sage'. It's got a great neckline, if you know what I mean. Throw those new cream trousers on that you came home with yesterday.'
'What about shoes?'
'Mmm, ah yes these strappy bronze sandals, you haven't worn them since last summer, at our party. Go on they're sexy. Perfect, you'll look gorgeous, darling.' The smile in Steve's voice was reassuring.
'Thank you, you are too kind. It's just, well, I haven't been out in ages. And look at the time now!'
'Look, you have to calm down Georgie. It doesn't matter if we're late, sorry, you're late. People are people, all of them our friends. Anyway, don't they say it's fashionable to be late.'
The words 'true, very true', massage my mind as I give myself the once over in our unforgiving full length mirror. It will have to do. I try to remember when smiling came easily. I really need to change the wattage in this room.

I arrive at 9.38pm, late but fashionably so. So, with customary bottle of wine, a dry white from New Zealand, I saunter up the driveway following the fairy lights, my luminary guides.
Classic Phil Collins is playing with gleeful streams of laughter bursting out at regular beats. Surprisingly, I feel at ease – calm almost.
'Ah Georgie, you're here, it's so good to see you! Let me take your things for you.'
'This is for you, Anne, happy birthday.'

'Thanks, Georgie, my favourite white, from the Marlborough region, you are a good mate. How are you anyway?'

'Good, yeah a lot better, thanks. I've even managed to stop the meds.'

'Wonderful, that's great news ... baby steps. It's been a horrible year, but I'm so very happy you made it tonight. You have to start interacting again, babe. Look, help yourself to anything, everyone is here, I've got to rescue some vol-au-vents from the oven.' Anne leaves after a quick kiss and embrace.

An hour has passed and I'm standing by myself, at the French doors gazing into the party at the party goers. Observing them but not being one. Detached and weary, even in a great neckline. I want to leave. Then I feel you near me. You whisper in my ear, 'I'm sorry I left you, left us, too early but remember my love, I'm with you, always'.

I dry my tears and join the others. The music has changed.

The Drawer

Clearing the house, I found an unopened envelope of photos.
Foon's Chemist Sylvia wrote in indigo bic blue. By touch there
    were many.
No doubt an assortment of images, so random not memorable.
Parakeets and Rosellas, fuzzy, in focus. Orchids in bloom.
Peace, Remember Me, and Just Joey, displaying their petalled
    perfection.
A myriad of cat shots. Tupps lying, jumping, posing, eating,
    sleeping.
Then one of us, my last visit. Your hand holding mine, like it
    knew it was the last time.

Anita Bodle

Nails

She's new. Better be good at fixing on nails.

She takes my right hand and without looking up says, 'Hello, I'm Elizabeth. Has it stopped raining?'

Here we go with the small talk I think to myself.

'Just about.' No answer.

Great, I think. We can skip the small talk after all.

'My boyfriend, well the man I was seeing, split up with me. A few days ago.'

I am rather shocked. Do some people really tell all to complete strangers?

'I'm bloody furious. Six months. He lied to me for six months. We had sex goodness knows how many times. Now I feel so bleeding dirty.'

She looks me straight in the eye. 'He used me, you see. He'd been unhappy with his wife for so long. He so desperately wanted to leave her.' She laughs. 'What a liar! I fell for his bloody sob story.'

I can't help but ask, 'And has he gone back to her now? Ouch.'

No reaction.

I hope her pent up anger won't cause me anymore pain.

'He never left her'.

After pausing for a moment she continues, 'He used to tell her that he was going away on business trips. Overnight stays.' Then she whispers, 'But he was with me.'

A shiver runs down my back.

She starts to file my new nails. 'He promised that he would be with me. And you know what? Like a fool I believed him. All I can say is, Alan Smedhurst, I hope you enjoy the dried up prune.'

She lets go of my hand, tries to take the other one but I push her hand away and clutch mine to my heart.

Well what's left of it. Do I detect a smile on those cheating lips. Does she know who I am.

I need to get out of here. Five talons in place. For what is to come.

Surgery

Nothing. Nothing makes sense. I'm here but not here.
I don't like my surroundings. And yet I do.
Blood was something I could never deal with, I'm sure.
And yet here I am working in an operating theatre.
Instructing everyone around me on what to do. Where did I learn
    all this.
Not from books that's for sure. I can't remember where.

Stitches. Then the man I have been working on is being attended
    to by the team who had assisted me.
Leaving the theatre I feel satisfied by the fact that my patient
    should now be free of pain.
And yet my pain will not go away.
I try my best to save people. To make their lives more comfortable.
I'm a well respected person.
But deep in me there is a young man, not particularly clever but
    happy and content.
A wife. Two children in his life.

I walk towards my car. Once in my flat I'll head straight for
    my bed.
Sleep, my way out.

Julie Evans

Some know some things

She knows he likes his black tea sweet
That he smokes Golden Virginia
His jeans are 34 inches in length
You can't find his size except in Levis
She knows how to bake him his favourite Battenburg
And that even though his family are Jews
He still eats bacon sandwiches in Cooplands café.
But what she doesn't know is why
He poured the hot coffee over her when she was asleep.

Luck

Bare trees arch over my head in my multi-coloured bobble hat as I walk kicking the remains of dirt brown leaves. A sleek black cat crosses my path.

It is an omen. I smile, feeling the smooth peel of the Cox's in my anorak pocket. I think of the sweet sour taste of its flesh.

A blue tit high in a Hawthorne is eating the last berries. I hear a miaow in the bushes, bend to look and find them.

Is this luck or is it more vet bills. Both, I decide.

Swing

At the bus station he swings back and forth, holding the rail,
Ignored by rows of passengers who have seen it all before.
His long thin legs stride out, up to Debenhams and back,
As his long hair swishes his face.
He speaks to no one, listens to no one, are we there at all?
Who waits for him, I think, at home,
Wherever home may be.
Wendi moves closer to the window as he sits down.
Afraid of what he will do. He is always a stranger. Always strange.

The Meeting

I sat on the rickety chair next to Frieda, her skin smelling of dust
    and chamomile.
From the corner of my eye I saw Joe looking at us. My feet shuffled
    on the old parquet floor, making marks in the dust.
I knew there were alliances here that had shattered like ice.
Mary shuffled her chair nearer to us, without a word.
A coffee mug banged on a table, sending droplets onto the pile
    of leaflets.
There was an audible muttering arising in a dark corner.
Then he pulled himself up, to stand on his one flesh leg.

Gwen Fletcher

Girl with the Pearl Earring

Everyone stops to look at me.
I sit on the lobe and wonder, if I moved slightly,
would it give a different slant on things.
But no, I'm quite content to stay put,
Knowing that all eyes are drawn to my soft sheen.
She might be the girl in the picture,
But I am the star of the milky way
and the sky is my limit.

A Good Send Off

Nora had set her alarm clock. She didn't need to, but she wasn't
  taking any chances.
She had the vol-au-vents to finish and the finger sandwiches to
  make.
She'd put those in the fridge wrapped in cling film, ready for Mrs
Evans who lived two doors down, to take out half an hour before
  the mourners got back from the funeral service.
She looked at the table set with her best china and the snowy
  table cloth.
She would give him a good send off.

It was nearly time for her to get changed, but first she went to
  the parlour.
This room got all the morning sun and had a lovely view.
Eric had always wanted to sit at that window with his pipe and
newspaper but she couldn't allow that. The parlour was for
  special occasions.
She went to the window and looked down into the coffin. Mr
Bailey the undertaker had done a lovely job on him, and think
how happy Eric would be now to end up in the parlour at last.
After all, it was a special occasion.

Addy Hall

I come from a big family and times were hard. Our dad left us and mam worked on the railways tapping lines.

One night when she was working, she looked up and saw a train coming.
It was almost upon her so she laid down flat between the lines, but a hooked chain caught her leg and dragged it round and round.

She was operated on for hours and the surgeon saved her leg, but she ended up wearing a plaster cast for eighteen months. And this is where a lovely lady came into the picture.

We lived in a village with a grocery shop that was owned by two spinster sisters. Addy (I presume it's short for Adelaide) ran the shop, whereas Ruth went out every day. She was very smart, she always wore gloves and a hat. I think she had a job. Addy was down to earth, and a little brusque but she had a good heart. She allowed my mam to run up a bill for goods for a long time until her compensation came through. She was a life saver.

She asked my mam if she would send one of our children to the shop on Christmas Eve and I was the one who was sent. When I got there she had an orange box ready. It had veg, fruit and nuts in, even some chocolate that was on ration then. I couldn't carry it home and had to run home to get my brother to help me.

We had a lovely Christmas thanks to Addy and I shall always remember this kind and trusting lady who helped my mam in her hour of need.

Orange Hat

I never looked good in a hat, but my sister Babs could wear
    anything on her head and look great.

She had an orange Kangol hat that she wore every Sunday when
    she went to the carboot.

She would wander off on her own and if I lost sight of her I
    would scan the crowds and look for a flash of orange.

Sadly, she passed away and her daughter gave me this hat.

It now hangs next to my mirror and I often pop it on. It brings
    back warm memories of Babs.

Kitt Dunn

Footwear

When I wear you on my feet, I traverse wild forest tracks and
    urban streets.
I've scaled the highest mountains, with Hannibal I crossed the
Alps, raided with the Sioux, and taken the white man's scalp.

I was there when General Gordon met his end at Khartoum.
Side by side with Armstrong, I walked upon the moon.
In Flanders field a different story, muck and bullets, death
    and glory.

I've been to Honolulu, Africa and Spain. When teatime calls
I'm homeward bound again. Are you a pair of stout, strong
boots that carry me over treacherous routes? No, just the pair
of worn out slippers I don, when I put my reading glasses on.

My Transport Through the Ages

I can't remember ever riding in a pram.

The first wheels I remember were on an old three wheeler, hand painted black with a wonky front wheel. Next came a sit-up-and-beg, no mudguards and a seat that moved up and down when you pedalled. We all shared this one and you had to be quick off the mark to stake your claim.
I worked on a farm for three years. I used to bring the horse and cart back to the farm at the end of a day's harvesting. I learned to drive a tractor during that time.
Working for Northern Dairies, I drove a milk float.
Then I worked on the buses as a clippie. I took the training for driving, but failed it because of my eyesight. I never did learn to drive a car.

But somewhere along the line, I do recall a soapbox trolley
my brother Jim knocked up with some old pram wheels he'd scrounged from somewhere.

Old Times

Seeing an old photograph of the old alms houses at Arksey
brought back memories of the times we lived in the old farm
house across from
All Saints Church.

I was four years old when we moved there, the house was
divided into two homes, No 7 and No 9, the High Street (9 was
demolished in 1958).
No central heating, the cooking was done on a large black cast-
iron range which had to be black-leaded every Saturday morning
with Zebra grate polish and the stone steps scrubbed and
donkey stoned. There was no hot running water, no electricity,
only gas light downstairs, upstairs was lit with oil lamps and
candles. The door was always open to cousins, uncles and aunts
who needed somewhere to stay.

During the war, soldiers (British and American) were billeted
in Arksey Hall, and German prisoners of war were sent to some
farms to work. To help with the war effort children went to
school half a day and the rest of the time went off to work in the
fields picking potatoes.

I went to Arksey school from 1937 to 1944. Mr Simmons, the
headmaster, was a real tarat. The large brass bell which called us
to lessons he used as a missile and would fling it across the room
at any boy who misbehaved and girls would get the black board
rubber across the back of the legs. We got no sympathy at home,
only 'You wouldn't get punished if you didn't do wrong'.

Entertainment: Hide and Seek, Whips and Tops, Marbles, Tin
Can Lurkey, Skipping and roaming the countryside far and
wide collecting wild flowers and picking blackberries. I can still
recognise birds by their song and flight.

Autumn brought conkers and bonfire night, each street trying to have the biggest fire and the best Guy Fawkes.

A penny or a clean jam jar would get us into the Coliseum in Bentley to cheer on Flash Gordon and the Claymen, Hopalong Cassidy, Roy Rogers and others.

There were other large families in the village, the Genders, Lowes, Atticks, Barlows and Slaters to name a few. We had some great times and battles when gangs were in fashion.

In summer we looked forward to the gala which was held in the field at the back of the church hall. (This now has houses – 'The Croft' – built on it.)

We had sad times too, like the time two boys' cousins drowned trying to sail across the pond at the Willow Garth. The loss shocked the whole village.

The post office was run by two spinsters, Miss Trout and Miss Hardcastle, and the grocery shop by two sisters, Addy and Ruth Hall, there you could knock on the side door and get served if you ran short of anything.

Hard times we had, wartime, and floods in 1947, but everyone was in the same boat. No trying to live like the Jones's, 'cos nobody had owt.

Chris Severn

The Ballad of Weasly Will

I've never told a soul before
but now I must confess
to something I did years ago;
I killed a man, no less.

I'd never been in trouble nor
done anybody harm;
a quiet man, I loved my work
with horses on the farm.

My mother came from farming stock
but sadly she died young
and I lost my inheritance
although I was her son.

I took to poaching in the woods
but then so did we all
for why should everything belong
to those up at the Hall?

Young Weasly Will saw my full bag
as I crept home one night
and when he tried to grab the sack
I knew we'd have a fight.

He punched and thumped and walloped me
then left me there half-dead.
With my last strength I dragged him down
and banged his weasly head.

But then I couldn't stop – I knew
that he'd go for the kill;
if one of us must die that night,
let it be Weasly Will.

I brought my spade and buried him
beneath a dry-stone wall
and hoped that nobody would miss
vile Weasly Will at all.

A search was made of fields and woods
but Will was never found
and I feigned total ignorance
when policemen called around.

But when the time for Hirings came
I thought I'd move away.
A Kirkbymoorside farmer said,
'You're good with horses – stay'.

My dreadful sin was always in
my mind, my soul, my heart.
I ended up with pleurisy,
sent home to die by cart.

The Great War came but my bad health
meant call-up passed me by.
In spite of having killed a man,
God didn't let me die.

I married, had a family,
kept working on the land
as shepherd, hedger, labourer
but nothing underhand.

I've kept my secret – had to do –
I feared the noose or jail,
but I'd like just one soul to know
so I've told you my tale.

Millie's Promise

I trod hard, city streets on soft, new paws
and stole dry bread from birds so I could eat.
On cold, wet nights I shivered out of doors;
in scary sunlight, hid from eyes and feet.
Soon I was caught and taught how to behave
with strokes and kindness but I still felt fear.
Then you came and I knew that I'd been saved –
my life of feline bliss was starting here.
I know I'm not the cat you hoped I'd be;
I don't need knees, I sleep at lofty heights.
By day I roam alone, wild and carefree,
back home with you, I sometimes hiss and bite.
I promise I might love you – we shall see.
But nowhere near as much as you love me.

Regrets

I couldn't believe what I'd just blurted out. How could I have been so stupid? Everything Sal and I had worked for, been through, planned to do; now I'd messed it all up.

I looked quickly round the room before I left: the long scratches on the brown, leather sofa from Mr Mogs' skidding claws, the oak sideboard we found that fitted exactly into the alcove, the faint mark from the splodge of sauce that had splattered onto the wallpaper just after I'd decorated. My own naïve face smiled optimistically from our wedding photo on the mantelpiece. The younger 'me' would never have said such a thing. Wisdom hadn't come with age.

My eyes settled on my mother-in-law, sitting like Lady Muck in my favourite armchair, closest to the fire. A superior smile played around her thin lips – it was tinged with satisfaction; she would be in her element. And she couldn't keep quiet.

'Told you so, Sal, I knew it would come sooner or later,' she crowed triumphantly. Her eyebrows had risen so high that they'd disappeared into her permed, grey fronds.

I didn't wait to hear what Sal had to say. I'd seen the shock on her face as I'd brushed past her and felt it in her stiffened arm. For the time being she was speechless and that was fine with me.

I managed to close the front door quietly but slammed the green, wooden gate viciously, leaving it swinging and banging on its rusty hinges. I looked at the black clouds that were gathering. Muttering angrily, I strode up the hill on the cracked paving stones, raised to all sorts of angles by the marauding tree roots; needing caution but as familiar as old, eccentric friends. By the time I got to the Rose and Crown, the rain had started but I felt slightly calmer and managed a grim smile for Phil, the landlord.

'My usual, please,' I said, weaving my way into the darkest corner.
What had I done? I propped my elbows on the sticky, ringed
table and put my head in my hands. It couldn't be unsaid.
Things would never be the same; what a fool I was.
Phil arrived with a frothing pint of bitter.
'What's up, mate?' He leant over me, concerned.
'You won't believe it,' I said through gritted teeth. 'I've just
asked Sal's mother to come and live with us.'

Carol Lee

Mervyn Fields

Epworth County Primary annexe, 1964. I've brought my doll that wees.

I take it to one of the sinks in the cloak room, pull its head off, fill it with water and *squeeeeze*. Mervyn's impressed, so I repeat it. After that we're almost inseparable.

Things progress quickly. We go from holding hands in the playground to exchanging dry kisses behind a propped-up Children's Encyclopaedia in class. Mr Bradbury catches us and blushes to the roots of his ginger hair.

Soon, Mervyn is escorting me home. I ride my bike, while he runs beside me. Then we call at his house to get his bike. I wait while his mum gets the steps and climbs up to get the small brown sweet tin from the top of the cupboard in the huge farmhouse kitchen. Mervyn and his two younger brothers are allowed to choose one sweet each. I stand back and wait. After Mervyn's checked every nut and screw on his bike and the tyres – his dad insists he does this for the outward and return journey *every* day – we're finally on our way. It's a two mile ride, and by the time we arrive at the Turbary, I've only got time to send him up the apple tree to nick us a Bramley – we didn't mind it being sour. Or maybe he'd take a photo of me sniffing a rose or something, with his dad's old camera, though he never had any film. Then it's time for him to get his spanner out, check his bike again, and off he'd go.

You can imagine our indignation then, when Aiden Cutforth spread terrible lies about us. He said he'd found us in a cornfield and I had not knickers on! Time passed, and soon there was talk of marriage. A blue camper van parked in his dad's field, that was the dream. It would have curtains of course, so that nobody could see us when we got undressed to have a wash. There was talk of two Alsatian dogs too, as I recall. But it was never to be ...

Carol Lee 61

Summer 1966

We're sitting under the pear trees. Lots of little hard pears are on the grass. Sometimes, if you pick one up that's been there a long time, there's a worm or a slug. If there's a centipede, I drop the pear quick. I don't like centipedes.

Before last playtime we were doing coil pots. I hope mine doesn't break in the kiln.
I'm sitting next to Mervyn Fields. He's got a pot on his arm again. Gillian Kuypers, in front of me, has got red checked ribbons in her plaits. Sometimes they're blue.

Mr Gudgeon is sitting on a chair, he's not got his jacket on today and he's propped his guitar against a tree. He tells us to stop chattering and starts to read a story about a man called St Francis. The book's got a picture of Jesus and some other people on the front. I'm picking clay from under my fingernails and Mr Gudgeon is telling us that St Francis was a man who liked spending a lot of time at parties and having too much fun, then he decides he wants to be nicer and he starts helping people. But the best bit is, the animals aren't frightened of him and they all come to him, if he stands still. When he sticks his hands out, birds perch on them. Mr Gudgeon showed us the picture.

When he's finished reading, Mr Gudgeon pushes the book in the top of his big brown bag and gets his guitar. We sing Puff the Magic Dragon and I can see my Mum waiting with the bike next to the hawthorn hedge.

When I run up to her, Mum lifts me up into the little metal seat and when we set off I press my cheek into her back, as she's told me to do.
We stop for a red lolly at Robinsons' and as I eat it on the way home I keep thinking about St Francis.

We're home. Mum lifts me out of the seat and, before she's even put the bike away, I'm running to the lawn. Then, making my face look as kind and holy as I can, I stick my arms out and wait for the birds to land on them and 'all the little animals of the forest' to stand around my feet. But nothing happens.

I notice Mum giving me a funny look as she walks back to the house. She's let Kip out and he runs to me but that doesn't count because he always does that anyway and he's only after drips of lolly on my shoe.

Well I've stood here long enough now, I'm starting to feel daft. I'm going to get some dandies for the guinea pigs.

George

Walking through Waterdale I see you. Brown checked jacket
out of shape, pockets pulled down through overuse. Baggy grey
trousers that look like they've fallen out with your shoes.

In my mind I can hear your gruff voice auctioning off at the
Harvest Festival. Now you're looking into shop windows
with the same rheumy eyes that used to look shiftily over the
congregation before we'd hear the inevitable 'That'll be mine
then', as you'd grasp the cake or whatever you'd been secretly
bidding for. You'd hold it between one hand and the stump at
the top of an empty sleeve or, which always seemed worse to me,
the hook you sometimes wore.

But now I feel foolish as I notice two full sleeves and remember
it must be twenty years since you died.

A Station in Surrey

This is what stays with me.

It's a still-sunny evening. I've left my friends and gone to catch a
    train back to London.

As I walk onto the platform I'm struck by the beautiful
atmosphere of this deserted sunny station. There are tall leafy
    trees on either side of the line.

The white painted cut work on the eaves of the station roof is as
    delicate as a doily.

I can hear nothing. I feel totally at peace. I could be anywhere.

This place has the feel of a deserted outpost in the old wild west.

When the train arrives to take me back to my dreaded workplace,
I expect cattle wagons, rattling, ramshackle and men in Stetsons.

Lace Attach

'You need a pair of tweezers,' says Gladys Hanratty, briskly. 'You can borrow mine for now, but you'll need to buy your own from the office, and some scissors.'

I look at the grey metal beast in front of me with its two cones of Gutterman thread. I soon understand the need for tweezers as, hands shaking under the impatient gaze of Gladys, I try time and again to feed the wayward thread through each eye, bar and tension. By the time I've threaded both needles I'm breaking sweat.

'Your job will be lace attach.' Gladys informs me, 'I'll show you how to thread the lace. You'll not have to waste any, mind. It's damned expensive.' She hands me a pile of Pantalettes and shows me how to work the lace through the rubber rollers. 'You'll need to tie your hair back before you start. There was a lass got hers taffled round the belt in Leicester. Scalped her.'

She hands me a small loop of elastic and I pull my hair into a pony tail then fasten it tightly. I feel my cheeks burn as I become aware of the old timers casting curious glances at the 'New Girl.' Each woman rocks rhythmically as she feeds the cloth in a continuous stream through the machine, foot never leaving the pedal.

Emma Butler

Girl In The Road

There's a girl in the road. The milk is spreading out into the cracks in the concrete, only now it's tinged pink where it trickles towards her tenpenny mix. My dad picks her up, though Mr Price tells him not to. But he's not thinking about whether she's injured her back, or how broken she is beneath her new tartan dress. He's only thinking that his daughter won't die in the road.

Mum hasn't moved from the kitchen floor since the lady next door came running. I wonder from my place at the table if she'll ever move again.

Grandad's Castor Oil

You cup my chin, for the second spoonful, finger and thumb. As
      if I'll pull away

the way he does, face twisted at the taste, until his back hits the
      pantry door. But

I don't mind it so much. Two quick swallows and the fresh
      rhubarb is already

cut by the sink, a bowl of sugar nearby. Later you'll brush the
      last of it from the

corner of my mouth with a smile. Honey slow Sunday with you.

The Difference Between Us

The time I moved for the fifth time in two years, and mum
walked us down the road with all of her pots and pans
drumming in a Silver Cross pram.
It's only just occurred to me to wonder whose pram it was,
because I was five and could walk all by myself, thank you very
much.

The time Sarah's keys had to be in by three O'clock, but when
I came after work at one she hadn't even packed. Drawers that
held everything from electric bill to batteries, Snowy's old collar,
a key to a forgotten door, all dumped in a bag and thrown in the
van. Mum still trapped in the cupboard under the stairs trying
to pack her way out. Up a rickety ladder at 2:55 getting Buzz
Lightyear out of the gutter, trying not to lean too far left or it's
infinity and beyond.

The time Glen tried to take a double bed down the stairs
without dismantling it first and got stuck three steps down. Two
hours of heaving and strategy, a new scrape in the plaster, tea
passed through the headboard slats. Until Dad had enough and
went to fetch his saw.

The time we moved into our first house, and you're Mr
Organised so everything is wrapped and packed and labelled
and going to the right room and it's nothing like I'm used to. My
family move like a hurricane, sweep it all up, drop it down, still
unpacking six months later, if ever. But you had the curtains up
by tea time, the kettle right where it was always going to be and
I'm home.

Cycling to the Moon

You will not remember the Saturday he woke at dawn in the bothy but didn't hitch the plough and tend to the back forty as he should have. Instead he walked the twenty miles to Kirkcaldy and paid a penny to see a man with a bicycle.

You will not remember that he was one of twelve brothers. How each in turn left the house at thirteen, their possessions tucked into a blanket chest made by their father, the promise of a job and a bed on the farm.

You will not remember how ten piped their way to the front. When it was the first time, when they would never believe we would repeat the same mistakes. You will not remember that only four came home.

You will not remember when he would drink whiskey with his youngest brother and always walk him home afterwards. How David would always walk him back again. Back and forth until a wife would get fed up and call them in to bed.

You will not remember that he lived to see a man walk on the moon.

You will not remember, but he's there behind the glass on the dining room wall. He's the Crawford on your keychain and your brother's middle name. He's in your blood and the colour of your eyes.

You will not remember him, but you know him just the same.

I'd like

I'd like to be in the window of your old house
when you painted it deep set with snow
I'd like to be the shadow behind frosted pane
stood sentinel in your lantern glow

I'd like to see the old well on the green freeze to glass
its midnight mirror lost to cloud
I'd like to take the smooth stone kept by the back door
cast it down and lift the shroud

I'd like to watch winter fade like low evening light
monochrome palette warm with the sun
I'd like spring to bleed through canvas with oils
that catch fire once summer's begun

I'd like to push at the boundary of the frame
touch walnut carved with Sunday care
I'd like to feel glass press me back
embraced in your yesterdays there

Ballad of the Barmaid

The lads all pile in at a quarter past five
after heeding the referees call.
First Jonno and Sully, Butcher and Jugs,
and right at the back Head the Ball.

'Good for nowt else,' when I asked the name,
'not like he'll go far in life.'
Sure seemed to me he was doing alright,
out the back with the club captain's wife.

Whispering Bill always nurses his pint,
sermonizing down into the rim.
Sotto voce cautions of hellfire and soul,
that only make sense if you're him.

Ambulance Annie from over the road,
a warning in pastels and pearls.
Had one too many on a long 'business lunch,'
and set fire to her bottle blonde curls.

Fishstick does his rounds at ten thirty,
offering a taste of the sea.
'Any crabs on yer, Cock?' the call from the back,
and everyone laughs, even me.

One of these days

after Julie Mellor

One of these days I'll pair up all the odd socks in the bag. Maybe
even go all out and throw them out if I can't find a matching
reindeer in a Santa hat. I'll tackle the black hole under her bed,
the one she thinks I don't know she tosses things into when she's
told to clean her room.

One of these days I'll learn how to talk to people. Without
the blushing. Without that voice in my head screaming, 'just
say something, anything will do at this point!' Without being
embarrassed when all I can come out with is, 'there's weather
today, I think ... outside.'

One of these days I'll live up to her. Her kindness, her patience,
her love. How she doesn't lose *her* temper fifteen times a day.
How easily she holds herself, like she's never been anyone else.
How she raised me. But then she tells me about the time she
forgot to put sun cream on the tops of my feet in the south
of France, and I blistered. And I think maybe I'll get there,
someday.

One of these days I'll invent a time machine and go back and
write down every story you told me. I won't fidget, or let my
mind wander to that to programme I wanted to watch. I won't
lose pieces of you I wish I'd fought harder to keep, because I
thought there would be more. I thought there would be time ...
and that was a mistake.

Rebecca Carpenter

Daffodils

'Surely there is nothing more that they can say', thought Lionel as he trudged to the shop, aware that for Alice Campion and Edith Garner, watching him provided yet another of their endless opportunities to judge what had happened. This time he heard only the name, 'Shirley', as he tried to concentrate on the cobbled road in front of him.

'I've said it before and I will say it again', Mrs Campion began the well-rehearsed litany 'he had it coming to him. Right from the start he put that child on a pedestal, not letting her play out with the other kiddies. What was she doing when she should've been playing hopscotch and running errands? And then, later on, do you remember him not letting her wear the same things as her school friends? Beryl was ashamed! What was he thinking of?'

Miss Garner knew that, at this point, she was required to present her response; a different side to the story, which would allow her friend to reinforce the strength of her own argument. 'Well. I don't know,' she hesitated, 'I think that Beryl had started to have a drink even before, well, you know ... It can't have helped, not having a wife like that ...'

'Well, that's the difference between us', Mrs Campion pronounced 'I do and you don't. Marriages are not always what they seem from the outside, or from those books you read. Beryl told me that ... well ... Lionel wasn't for that sort of thing, not after Shirley, anyway, and if she did have the odd sherry in the afternoon, who could blame her? What I am saying is, that he spoilt Shirley. Everyone knew that Shirley reckoned that she was better than the rest, and she thought that everybody worshipped her. If she'd been mine, things would have been a bit different, I can tell you.'

She wouldn't have been dead, anyway, thought Miss Garner, although she considered it best not to open up that aspect to Mrs Campion, quite yet.

Miss Garner couldn't bear to hear her friend dissect the details of finding Shirley lying in a pool of blood, not pure red blood, like she'd thought at first, when Alice had told her, but blood with ... Alice was right, the romances she got from the lending library didn't end like that.

Knowing that the women could not leave what had happened alone, Lionel wondered whether he did need to say more. Shirley had been a miracle, a gift, he had wanted to protect her. He had made sure that she went to Church, went to Sunday-School. He remembered her taking the bunch of bright daffodils that she had bought with her pocket money to the Sunday-School teacher, the yellow of the flowers had lit up Shirley's face.

Lionel had known that things were starting to go wrong when Beryl had encouraged Shirley to join the youth club. He had felt himself losing control after Brian had started going there too. Shirley had begun to spend time at Brian's house; Beryl had encouraged this – his family were the sort that Beryl admired. It wasn't just the television in the lounge that Brian's father, Alan, had bought on the never-never, it was the evenings down the club with him and Phyllis; the table in the corner seemed only to seat the five of them. Shirley wasn't keen to talk to him about Brian, and by the autumn she had seemed reluctant to go round to Brian's house, or to the club, despite Beryl's pleading. In the end, to his relief, Beryl had gone on her own without Shirley; perhaps a table for four had been found.

That January day, the seventh, a Friday, Shirley had started back at school. It was to be her last term at school, before she started work. Lionel had got her a position in the office where he worked. Things had been difficult over Christmas, Shirley hadn't wanted to go out, and she hadn't wanted to see any-one.

Rebecca Carpenter 75

Beryl had done nothing but have a go at her: she was mardy, she was miserable, she was a spoilsport, she was a lump of lard ... Lionel had failed to cheer Shirley up, it was true that she had been putting on weight – too many selection boxes he had thought – he had always bought her too many things. He remembered coming home and seeing the curtains drawn, not that that in itself was unusual. He had tried to open the door, but it was locked and the key was on the inside.

Banging on the door and raising his voice had not brought Beryl, but had summoned an excited Mrs Campion who was only too willing to tell him that she had seen Beryl, in town, going in to the Horse and Trumpet; her pursed lips had suggested, but not revealed, the name of Beryl's companion. Lionel had been forced to break a window in the scullery to let himself in. When he had switched on the light he had seen Shirley on the floor, the blood was still wet, the knitting needle was half obscured by her body curled up as she had been as a baby.

Beryl had left not long afterwards, driven away with Alan in his new car. She had not left without a few choice remarks to the neighbours, creating an image of a guilty father to blame for both a dead daughter and a heart-broken mother. Lionel thought that the carefully selected words had provided a smoke screen for her own behaviour.

Much later, Lionel had sorted through Shirley's things, packing her clothes carefully in tissue paper into the suitcase she had taken when they had gone on holiday. Placing her hardly worn shoes back into their box he had found her diary. At first he hadn't wanted to read what she had written, but then he felt that he needed to know what had happened to his beautiful little girl.

Lionel had packed it away with her dolls, it could have been a story which she had written, a composition for school. It didn't seem real ... who could do that to his bright little star? What would Mrs Campion and Miss Garner make of that? More to the point, what would Beryl think of Alan now?

'William. Bill or Billy'

William. Bill or Billy, but never Jessica
Inhabited a future for six, ten and once for twenty weeks
Smiling, suckling, smelling of milk
Standing to attention in a cub cap, saluting the Queen
Riding down the road on his 11+ bike.
A boy, of course, all the Clarkes were boys
Except those who were not.

A brother, an older brother, not a girl
'Don't do that to my sister.' How might that have been
in the playground, the pub, in the living room?
Driving a car back from the university
Sharp suited management at the works
Excelling. All the Clarkes were good at maths
Except those who were not.

I stare warily from the photo frame
Hair cropped around my ears, the school shirt and tie
Secondary Modern Badge, the regulation blazer
Domestic Science, needlework and typing.
'If only you had been a boy.' I let him down,
Failing to be the one the Clarkes wanted
Being what they were not.

Kath Johnson

Watching

I went by the house the other day
and I saw her, peering out
into her ever dimming world
from the comfort of her big red chair.

The house is changed, new curtains,
paint and pots, new kitchen furniture
and lots of flowers swaying in the sun.
I went by the house the other day.

And what they do not know
is she's still there, her tiny frame
encompassed in the big red chair.
Scrutinizing. Always on the watch.

What a Difference an Hour Makes

There was no one in the office when she arrived. Glenys arrived an hour later, but didn't say anything except, 'Good Morning.' Barbara knew she'd been having a tough time lately. The rumour was Glenys had split with her long-time partner. That she was having to look after the baby alone, and finding life hard. Not that she mentioned any of it to her. Wonder why we've never got on, thought Barbara. We seem to have a lot in common. Same age, similar interests, but Glenys never confided in her.

Barbara was in the washroom when she overheard two of the junior girls talking.

'Glenys is so upset,' stated Moira.

'I know,' replied Patsy. 'He promised he was going to leave her but he's still not done it. Not even told her that he's been seeing Glenys. Coward.'

So Glenys has another man, thought Barbara. A married one at that.

Barbara looked at her watch. Lunchtime. She slipped her arms into her coat, and picked up her bag. Then noticed Glenys doing the same. Funny thought Barbara, she usually takes her lunch an hour after me.

It was as she was coming out of the bank that Barbara saw them. Sat on a bench in the square, arms wrapped around each other, kissing.

Barbara didn't go back to work that afternoon. Instead she returned home.

It was after she had rung the locksmiths, and packed her husband's bags before depositing them on the doorstep, that she sank onto the sofa with a large glass of Chablis. She turned on the news. She was an hour too early. Then she remembered, she had forgotten to alter the clock last night.

She turned off the TV, and nestled back into the cushions, breathing in the peace.

Barbara smiled. Oh how she hoped the baby cried all night.

Her Next Door

Outside the gate at number 39
'Hello Gladys, not seen you for a bit, how are you?'
'Not so bad except for me knees, how are you, Freda?'
'Glad I've had me hip done and I can get round again. Did you know we've got new neighbours? Eee Gladys, have you seen her?'
'Ooo I have.'
'The stuff she wears.'
'Don't know who she thinks she is. Where's she come from?'
'The leafy suburbs. Leafy suburbs, I ask you'.
'What's she mean by that?'
'God knows. She's split up with her husband, you know.'
'No wonder, 'cause she seems to have an eye for't men.'
'Oh don't I know it. He were glued t'window the other day, what are you looking at Bert I said, ooo, he said he was looking at his roses, roses I ask you, when I went to look there she was bending over, skirt hardly covering what it ought.'
'Ooo I say, what was she doing?'
'Snipping away with some clippers at what she calls her topiary.'
'Whatever's that?'
'She's got some bits o' green in plant pots, and she snips at em and makes them into animals, squirrels and rabbits an' the like.'
'What for?'
'God knows. She says it's therapeutic, takes her mind off things. She'd be better off if she went in and cooked them kids a good dinner. I bet there's nowt much on that table.'
'Wouldn't be surprised. I saw takeaway man going there other day delivering pizzas. All that fancy foreign muck's no good to them kids, they need some proper meals.'
'I agree.'
'What did you say she's called?'
'Chastity, Chastity I ask you.'
'Chastity? By, that's a joke.'

'That's what I say, I said to Bert, I bet she's made that one up.'
'Eee I don't know Freda, it's a funny old world, not like when we were young.'
The door opens at number 37
'Oh hello Chastity love, how are you this morning?'
'Fine Freda, fine.'
'This is Gladys from t' next street. I was just telling her what lovely new neighbours we'd got. Don't forget love if there is anything you need you only have to ask.'

That October

Do you remember that October when we tramped the lanes,
scuffing through banks of leaves, before laying on damp grass
in the last gasps of the summer sun.

Do you remember the evenings when a hint of sparkle
decorated almost empty branches, when blinds were drawn and
you lit the logs.
Do you remember the dreams we spun as we watched sparks fly
the chimney.

Now, as October returns and the days shorten, and fields wake
wrapped in mist,
you look through vacant eyes at blood red leaves rotting on
damp grass, flickering walls and decorated branches, your
dreams forgotten.

I see your tired face, and how I wish you could remember that
October.

Anne Aitchison

E D Robertson

'It wasn't much, this urge to disguise and deceive. After all, great playwrights and directors through history have employed this technique. You know what I mean. For a start there's a film that employs scary music, sinister landscapes, rising tension in the form of wolves howling or footsteps following you. And then, just when you think you can't stand any more and you make a break for the kitchen, the playwright/director employs a master stroke. Magically, the wolves are in a zoo and the footsteps following you are those of the harmless neighbour out walking his dog. As for the scary music, that disintegrates into a cacophony of humorous piccolo squeals and somehow, you feel cheated out of the terror you didn't want to experience in the first place.

You see, my dear, once you have sanitised terror and fear, taken away that elemental "fear of the unknown", you have committed a cardinal sin. That is, the opportunity to be frightened witless in the comfort of your own home. Then, if you don't provide a satisfactory denouement, you've cheated your audience again. They expect to be afraid if you employ all the usual tricks. Your job is to be a bit more sophisticated about it. "The Creature from the Blue Lagoon" just won't do nowadays. Like Agatha Christie, you need a whole shoal of red herrings, placed in exactly the right spot at the right time.'

With that, she put down her empty glass and, with a 'Must be going now. Good luck with your enterprise' she collected her hat and coat and quietly let herself out of the flat.

He came to quite abruptly as the rain subsided and the lounge window reflected in the street light below. He picked up the faded photograph of his mother, taken just before she passed away in 1972, the celebrated writer, E D Robertson, and hoped he could live up to her memory. Getting up from the armchair, he thought he could detect the scent of Palma Violets. Smiling, he remembered, it had been a favourite of hers.

The Expressionistas

There again, in the same place, same time
to-ing and fro-ing, machines
except they weren't machines
machines have no expression
or blank expression
or expression we make up
for them

These had expression
but not the type you recognise
the to-ing and fro-ing
the zooming, the rubber burning
and the digging and flinging and examining
all of it beyond comprehension

Except they accomplished something
What were they and why?
Why did they stop
in a line, silent, waiting
looking left, right, straight ahead
each head blazing with a yellow light
then fading, fading to a weak gleam

The Hat

When he wore that hat,
that matched his suit
When he conformed,
I wept and stopped listening

And then Suzanne deigned
to haunt his melody again
And I turned away
Wiser, calmer now

The flame extinguished
by the hat that hid the man
The shock of grief and death and love

But underneath that hat
his voice dark as coffee,
damaged, attacked
and bitten by commerce

Still he held me for a while
and I smile
as I remember him
young, cool and certain

My Innisfree

I knew what to expect. I had the book, the words that mattered.
Everything else was secondary, even the crossing and the train
journey. The sun leant an extra glow to my high expectation.
Then the sky darkened and wind rattled the windows. Someone
snapped one shut, impatient. Buried in my book, I didn't hear
steady drizzle inching its way down the glass. We lurched to a
stop. There was a flurry of coats, bags, doors opening, the nasal
tones of the guard propelling us from the train.

Half way to the island, the drizzle turned serious. I fixed my
eyes on the approaching shore line. It was green and lush but
not particularly welcoming. I was cold with the wind full on
my face. Clutching his book to me I started to recite the first
verse. Reluctantly, but then with more gusto, the others joined
in. The words, having a mind of their own, ripped away from
the little boat and scattered themselves over the rolling waves,
making their way towards landfall and the small cabin of clay
and wattles. This was to be our home for the next few days.

By nightfall, we had made a fire in the grate and sat round eating
and drinking in its warm glow. Outside, the wind howled and I
wondered about the nine bean-rows and the hive, whether they
would be safe. Then, just before midnight, the wind abated.
My bed was by a window. I pulled back the curtains to watch
the moon. I was in exactly the right position to see the Corona
Borealis, the miniature tiara given to Ariadne by Bacchus.

Outside, the lake ebbed and flowed reflecting the stars of that
exquisite tiara and I slept, curtains still wide, dreaming of linnet's
wings and a bee-loud glade.

Happy Freedom

The pen lies still, it's lifeless now
Alone and out of touch
A pain-wracked leaf of paper stands
A testament to much

The book's agape, cast aside
The chair is set askew
A dirty cuff and smudge of ink
What is this? I ask you

For ballad's died and sonnet too
McGough, he hangs his head
MacMillan swears and eats his words
And Pam has lost her head

For now the future beckons us to think instead of rhyme
And all the world's not Shakespeare's stage
It's merely out of time (and meter)

Stella Mathers

Promise

You made me a promise
You hid it in seeds,
Shaped it in rainbows,
In the tracery of leaves,
In the deep life of oceans,
In the heights of the tarn,
In the dust of the moon,
In the fire of the star,
In the flight of the geese,
In the cry of the young.
You made me a promise,
That I would go on.

The Weight

It sits between us where it's always been.
Like a huge lump of wet clay thrown onto a board.
Like a massive piece of marble.
Like a heavy door slammed shut.
Immovable.
Unyielding.
Unforgiving.
Just there.
The thought of the task wearies us.
Are we willing to try?
Let's both give our hands and our strength.
To slowly,
Persistently,
Push.

Oh My Days!

Ordinary day,
I put the clothes away,
Clear the sides,
Sweep the floor,
Exactly like the day before.

Ordinary things,
Photo frames and rings
I polish 'til they
Glint and shine,
Reflecting on this life of mine.

Ordinary me
Is all that you can see.
Friendly face,
Smiling eyes –
I'm good at wearing that disguise.

An ordinary lie
Writes I'll be back by nine.
My suitcase full,
I turn to go.
I leave the casserole on low.

Kath Lightfoot

The Delivery

I answered the knock at the door and my heart froze. I recognised the small brown parcel in the postman's hand. So many of my neighbours had lived this moment before me. I signed for it, hand shaking, eyes blurred.

'Are you alright, missus?' Concerned sympathy showed in the postman's eyes and voice. He had delivered so many of these parcels to so many families.

I sat in *His* chair gazing into the fire. It was one of his favourite pastimes as a very young child, making fire pictures. Castles, volcanoes, shipwrecks, they were all there in his imagination. All I can see is shell holes, trenches and that hell called The Somme. My chest is so tight. I could hardly breathe as I remembered the words on that telegram. Missing – presumed dead and then later – no known grave.

His boots stand side-by-side on the hearthstone. I can't bring myself to move them. They were my act of faith, my touchstone. They would be ready waiting for him when at last he came home. He always sat on the back step, whistling, as he blacked them and my mind's eye cherishes his quick smile, the set of his head, his hands. Its all I've got left of him, memories, a pair of boots and a ladder of birthday notches carved on the outhouse door.

Just like his mates, he couldn't wait to go to war. What did the papers say? – Work together – fight together. Aye, and this street and town know the consequences of that stupidity.

I opened the parcel. Two medals and a brass memorial plaque, not much to show for a young life. A brass plaque for our golden lad. There's a slip of paper — The King wishes me — gave his life that others might live. The grief, anger and loss chokes me. I didn't notice any of your sons, George, being led by donkeys in Flanders mud, with trench-foot, shell shock, or making the supreme sacrifice.

The only consolation I can cling to as I struggle with the tears is that no one else will suffer this pain. That this was the war to end all wars.

Ann Sansom

Psalm For Those Who Go Forth On Tuesday Mornings

For they rise up early and drink weak tea, or leave the bag in
or go half with whiskey if they have a cough, according to their
    own nature

And they clean their house in readiness for guests, or they go
    clear off, you guests
And other rude language. For they are women who have come
    to an understanding

And they, according to their vows and rightly filled in and
    signed WEA forms
venture out in all weathers, and set their face willingly against all
    manner of flood and storm

and bad leg and bad back and night-shift and hangover and
    diverse other ailments
which mean nothing to them for they have given their word and
    their friends rely upon them

And they are of good cheer for the kettle is on and Kitt has
    delivered the milk
and they rap on the Minster window, shouting ey up, let us in or
    missed my bus and otherwise

and they year on year overcome all manner of trouble and woe
    and stolen bike
and mislaid specs, for they are of good faith and have
    determined to enter

and they rinse grapes, lay out biscuits and they write that which
    is according to their nature

whether it be prose or poem or play or song. And yes, often it is
     song

which is sung in that room, as laughter is sung, and that which
     comes to tears is sung,
and everything which is spoken privately between friends is
     sung. And we rejoice

and then go to our separate houses, rejoicing because we have
     friends in this world
and we may, regardless of our vices, meet on Tuesdays and raise
     our voices

For this we give praise